Release

Your

Potential

by
Rosalie Marsh

Christal Publishing

CHRISTAL PUBLISHING
11, Briarswood, Rhosrobin, WREXHAM, LL11 4PX.
www.christalpublishing.com

Cover Design © Christal Publishing.
Images © Rosalie Marsh.
www.discover-rosalie.com

First published 2011 by Christal Publishing.
ISBN 978-1-908302-08-3

Also available as an e-book.

British Library Cataloguing in Publication Data. A catalogue record for this book is available from the British Library.

This book is printed on acid-free paper.

Contents

Introduction.

This second in the Lifelong Learning: Personal Effectiveness series is intended to help you to wade through all the forest of information you may have been reading about Lifelong Learning, Personal Development, and Continuing Professional Development (CPD) etc. The list goes on.

It can seem a bit scary, especially if you are not working in an organisation, which sets a lot of store in developing its staff to improve and raise standards. You may be in an organisation, which *does* actually invest a lot of time and effort in its workforce; in which case you are very lucky.

On the other hand, you may not even be in work at the moment and think to yourself:

'This book isn't for me but I do want to do something with my life!', as you are about to put it back on the shelf or close your browser (if you are searching on-line).

STOP! Don't go away! Read on! Because whatever situation you are in; whatever level you are at in life, I want to help you to go that little bit further and achieve a little more. In other words – make the best of yourself.

As with many things in life, it is not enough to declare that, you can do this or that. You have to have some proof or evidence that you can actually do something; that you have actually done what you claim to have done.

'So how do I do that?' I can hear you say.

Simple. You keep a record. It can be a very simple list on one sheet of A4 paper or it can be a more detailed record.

This is called a Continuing Professional Development record or CPD record.

What I am going to show you in the pages of this book is a little more than 'professional development'. I am going to show you how things you do in your personal life are just as important in releasing your potential and developing your 'whole person'.

Apart from saying that learning *is* lifelong I am not going to define what lifelong learning means as that is covered in *Lifelong Learning: A View From the Coal Face*; the first book in this series of personal effectiveness guides. All I will say is that we are learning all the time; that learning is lifelong from the day when you took your first breath, your first steps, said your first garbled words, kicked your first ball, learned how to dress your dolls, played with your friends (teamwork) and spent about eleven years in formal education.

If you have just left school or university, you may think:

'That is it. I know it all now.'

Can I shatter that illusion? Your real learning journey is just starting. You have the foundations from your school days. Now, you have your whole life ahead of you to grow and develop, to release, realise, and achieve your potential as you develop your whole person.

Continuing Personal and Professional Development.

In addition, you must obtain the skills and knowledge needed for the future. This means constantly learning new processes as technology and economic needs change. This is your responsibility. If you are fortunate, your organisation will be investing in its workforce – as many do.

In other words, you are managing your life.

You will ask yourself:

> - Where am I now?
> - What are my strengths & weaknesses?
> - Where do I want to be?
> - What are the opportunities & threats?
> - How do I get there? Which route do I take?
> - What am I going to need? Development? Experience?
> - Do I have what is needed?
> - Opportunities – how will I get them?
> - How am I going to get involved?
> - Do I change my job?
> - Threats – what will stop me doing what I need to do?
> - What other action should I take?
> - What daily activities do I take part in that will help me to get to where I want to go?
> - What current resources are there in my organisation or another one?

The Way Forward.

Join me in the journey as we decide:

- ➤ How to compile a simple Curriculum Vitae or C.V.
- ➤ How to complete a S.W.O.T. Analysis.
- ➤ What I know now.
- ➤ What I need to know in the future.
- ➤ How I will learn what I need to know.
- ➤ What will stop me doing this?

Then we will move on to:

- ➤ How we decide which is the best way forward for *you as an individual* to learn.
- ➤ How we manage our time.
- ➤ How we manage our stress levels.

I will show you:

- ➤ How to draw up and complete a Personal Action Plan.
- ➤ Keep a record of what you have done and need to do to keep focussed on your objectives.
- ➤ How to set aside time to look back on what you have done and see how far you have travelled.

In this way, as you take responsibility for your learning and development you will see yourself gradually improve and grow in confidence as you break down the barriers; climbing the ladder to where you want to be – and become a winner.

You must keep up to date and plan for the future. The days of a job for life have long since gone.

Winners and Losers.

A **Winner** looks up to where he is going.
> A Loser looks down on those who have not yet achieved the position he has.

A **Winner** says 'I'm good but not as good as I ought to be.'
> A Loser says 'Well, I am not as bad as a lot of other people.'

A **Winner** makes mistakes and says 'I was wrong.'
> A Loser says 'It wasn't my fault.'

A **Winner** knows what to fight for and what to compromise on.
> A Loser compromises on what he/she should not and fights for what is not worth fighting for.

A **Winner** is responsible for more than his/her job.
> A Loser says 'I only work here.'

A **Winner** works harder than a loser works and has more time.
> A loser is always 'too busy', thus staying a failure.

A **Winner** credits his / her good luck for winning, even though it was not luck.
> A Loser credits his/her bad luck for losing even though it was not luck.

A **Winner** says 'There ought to be a better way of doing it.'
> A Loser says 'Why change it? That's the way it has always been done.'

(Anonymous)

Compiling a Curriculum Vitae.

A Curriculum Vitae is simply a structured record about your work, life, and achievements, which are listed in a chronological order.

This guide is aimed at a variety of levels and abilities. It is for you the reader to pick out what suits you; what can help you to improve; or what you find you could do differently.

Therefore, I make no apologies if some of you find parts of this a little basic as it is surprising how many people have worked their way up in their jobs without any formal training on this subject.

As it is important to have at least a basic up-to-date Curriculum Vitae or C.V. easily accessible, we will build an evaluation of yourself as a person into the Personal Profile part of a C.V. as we go along. You will then be able to work towards compiling or updating your C.V. If you do not have one, now is the time to put one together.

I have put together a set of tasks to make this process easier. You will need a notepad and pencil to make notes and jot down your thoughts. Keep all your notes – you will need them later.

There is a space to write in the gaps if you prefer to do that.

Task 1

Identify 10 positive words to describe yourself.

....

....

....

....

Identify 10 negative words to describe yourself.

....

....

....

....

Task 2

Look again at the Winners and Losers checklist in the previous chapter. Do any of these apply to you? Are you a Winner or Loser? It would perhaps be a good idea to build the more positive ones into your personal profile for your C.V.

Prospective employers see this section first so it must have impact. It must ensure that the person scanning the applications will put *your* C.V. in the 'must see' pile and be included in the short list.

Task 3

Using the example in the sample C.V. overleaf, construct a short sharp 'profile' using your 10 positive words. The rest can be filled later but remember there is no need to put your date of birth, your marital status or how many children you may or may not have. It is your suitability for the job, which matters.

Do not put any confidential information, such as your National Insurance Number, under any circumstances as you could lay yourself open to identity theft.

Are you are a member of a professional organisation (e.g. you may be undertaking a qualification which gives you affiliated membership such as the Institute of Leadershship and Management)? If so, it is well worth including this on your C.V. – even though affiliated status does not normally allow you to put designated letters after your name – as it demonstrates your commitment to your development and upskilling. If you have achieved a qualification, which allows you to join a professional organisation, again I would advise you to do so. The organisation will tell you if there are any designated letters, which you can put after your name. It is important to include any which are applicable as this demonstrates that you are up to date. Professional organisations normally have a periodic journal, which they send to members with articles, which keep them up-to-date with issues in their area of work.

(At the time of writing, these professional membership fees are tax deductable.)

It is important that you have all your work and education properly laid out and updated on a regular basis.

This not only allows you to have a snapshot in front of you of what you have done; it is handy to have one to hand when a suitable position comes up, especially if the deadline is close.

If you are just setting out on your career path – you may have just left school – your C.V. may be quite basic. Do not worry about this. Write about yourself and what you have done. If you have someone who can help you, then ask them. Very often, other people can see qualities in you that you either don't or would be too shy to put down on paper.

Curriculum Vitae of < Name >.

(Also, add any professional designatory letters after your name or a degree.)

Personal Profile. *(Example)*

I am an organised, enthusiastic, and committed individual who has demonstrated accomplishments in the areas of *<here put whatever relates to you>*.

I am a motivated individual with good communication skills and a flexible attitude who works well in a team. I have contributed in a positive way to the work of my department *< give an example if possible>*. Recently I have *<here insert something positive you have done>*. My current position as a *< . . . >*, requires me to apply method, attention to detail and interpersonal skills. In my spare time, I am a member of my local amateur dramatic society, which relies on teamwork.

Personal Information.

| Address: | e-mail: |
| Tel: | Mobile: |

Professional Memberships. *(If none, leave out.)*

| June 2008 – to date | Institute of Leadership and Management. Member. |

Education. Training. Professional Qualifications.

Date: (most recent first)   Awarding Body and subject.

If you are working towards a qualification, include this before anything you have already achieved. If you are undertaking an apprenticeship which has lots of different parts (e.g. the Technical Certificate or taught part of the course which provides the knowledge and understanding or the NVQ/Key Skills etc.) then list the name of the Apprenticeship and then all the components.

Don't forget to list your GCSE and GCE A-level results — highest grade first.

Include any achievements from school e.g. Princes Trust Award/Duke of Edinburgh Scheme/Health and Safety or First Aid Certificates.

Employment Experience. *(Most recent first.)*

Date: **Organisation. Address. Position.**

This involved — *(Here give a general overview of your duties.)*

Achievements. *(Here give any successes your department achieved or targets you reached. Include your personal contribution.)*

Date: **Organisation. Address. Position.**

This involved — *(Here give a general overview of your duties.)*

Achievements. *(Here give any successes your department achieved or targets you reached. Include your personal contribution.)*

If it is not long since you left school or worked, do not forget to include any part-time or casual work. What you include in this section depends on your circumstances.

If you are further on in your working life you may want to make the earlier positions briefer.

If you have had a number of part-time or short-term jobs, you could combine them all together by saying for instance:

1998 - 2003 I worked in a variety of jobs in . . .

This would show that you are flexible and willing to work.

Personal Interests and Activities.

Here you could include any clubs or organisations of which you are a member. This helps to give your prospective employer a brief insight into you as a person and what other qualities you demonstrate that you could bring to the job role.

References are available on request.

Do not include references unless the job description asks for them. These will be asked for if the employer wants them.

Signature: Date:

Include a footer in the document with the date so that you know when it was updated.

You now have the basis of your own Curriculum Vitae (C.V.). Of course, you are free to construct yours in any way that you wish. The guidelines above are, however, tried and tested.

We will re-visit this later on when you begin to put together your Personal Development Portfolio.

S.W.O.T. Analysis.

Strengths. Weaknesses. Opportunities. Threats. (S.W.O.T.)

A S.W.O.T Analysis is not as frightening as it sounds. It is simply looking your strengths and weaknesses, what opportunities you have for learning and any threats that may stop you achieving what you have set out to do.

Keep that notepad and pencil to hand so that you can make some notes at various points in the topics.

To begin the process of evaluating yourself, you need to identify what skills and qualifications you already have.

To assess your strengths and weaknesses (or areas for development as I prefer to call it), complete the 'Personal and Work Skills Stock take' on the following pages.

Personal Skills	Can do	Can do with help	This is difficult
Work on my own.			
Work with other people as part of a team.			
Thank people for their help.			
Organise and prioritise tasks.			
Keep a check on progress of tasks.			
Ask for help if I have a problem.			
Apologise if I am wrong.			
Accept feedback.			
Express my views clearly, and calmly.			
Listen to and respect other people's views.			
Think about a task before rushing in to start it.			
Good time keeping.			
If I am late or sick I telephone ahead.			
Respect other people.			
I am polite, helpful, and flexible.			
I am always clean and tidy in my dress.			

Work Skills	Can do	Can do with help	This is difficult
I make notes when I am researching for information.			
Discuss my work.			
Write about myself clearly.			
Take part in discussions and listen to other views.			
I know how to find information from different sources.			
Use a telephone.			
Accept responsibility.			
Keep to a timescale for tasks.			
Respond to challenges.			
Put away documents/papers/ equipment neatly & quickly.			
Persevere when things get difficult.			
Follow health & safety rules.			
Use a computer.			
Receive and send e-mails.			
Research the Internet.			
Use word processing software.			
Can do simple calculations without a calculator.			
Know how to use images in documents.			
Check my work for accuracy.			

For the **Personal Skills** checklist, add up how many ticks you put under –

Can do.

Can do with help.

This is difficult.

For the **Work Skills** checklist, add up how many ticks you put under –

Can do.

Can do with help.

This is difficult.

You will now have an idea of where you need to improve. I hope that you will have many 'Can do' ticks.

It is not easy admitting that you fall short in certain areas. However, you may be surprised at some of the more positive qualities you have. Ones which you may not have considered to be important or worth mentioning on a C.V.

In the light of this, you may want to go back to your Personal Profile and re-do it. It often takes a couple a drafts before you can get it right.

It is also sometimes useful to ask someone else what they think. You might be surprised at their perception of you.

Another outcome of completing these checklists is that you will perhaps realise where you need to improve or increase your skills before you apply for jobs, which are not suitable – at this time.

I have said – *at this time* – as there is nothing to stop you working towards being suitable in the future.

Remember, learning is a series of building blocks.

Learning Techniques.

In this section, we will look at some of the ways, which will help you to learn. Some of the ways, which will suit you as an individual best.

Learning techniques are things and ways, which help you to learn better and more effectively.

If you know *how* to learn effectively, and more importantly, how you *like* to learn, you will find learning far more enjoyable. The reward for your efforts will be far greater. You will achieve.

We are all different. Some of us like to have music playing to help us to concentrate while some of us prefer to sit in total peace and quiet as we lose ourselves in the subject.

However, the main areas you should concentrate on are given below. Answer each question carefully – then work out the areas in which you need to change your habits in order to learn effectively.

In the following chapters, we will look at how you can improve and manage these areas so that you can increase your skills and employability.

Do you use your time to the maximum advantage?

Y /N

Could you improve your time management?

Y /N

Can you write notes quickly and accurately which cover the main points and understand them later?

Y /N

Can you find notes months later?

Y /N

Could you improve your note writing?

Y /N

Do you expect to be able to learn information just by reading?

Y /N

Can you improve the way you digest what you read?

Y /N

Can you clearly identify the different ways in which you would read a telephone directory, a recipe, a novel?

Y /N

Do you think they are all the same?

Y /N

Do you recognise how you can learn from other people?

Y /N

List some different ways. Use your notepad or write in the space overleaf.

Other Ways of Learning.

Completing a S.W.O.T. Analysis.

You will have identified what qualities you already have and what you need for your chosen career or even where you would like to improve in your personal life.

Where do you want to be in 1 yrs time?

....

....

....

Where do you want to be in 3 or 5 years time?

....

....

....

You now have the first part of the S.W.O.T. Analysis.

Strengths.

What are your current **strengths** that you would like to develop or the areas of work you enjoy?

....

....

....

How will you make the most of these?

....

....

....

Weaknesses. (Areas for development.)

What areas did you define as **weaknesses** or things you could improve on? (This could be as simple but as important as bad time-keeping and missing targets.)

....

....

....

How can you develop or overcome these?

....

....

....

Opportunities.

Now think about *what* opportunities there are to enable you to do what you want to do.

These will be short term (1 year) and longer term (5-10 years).

I know that this seems a long time but it was only by thinking this far ahead and planning my route, that I actually achieved what I wanted to do a few years earlier when an opportunity presented itself.

....

....

....

What **opportunities** are there to my achieving my goals or my plan? *Who* will help me? *Where* will I learn new skills?

....

....

....

How can I make the most of these opportunities?

....

....

....

Threats.

What **threats** are there to my achieving my goals or my plan?

....

....

....

How will I overcome and minimise these?

....

....

....

(A threat to your plans could be something as simple as being able to get to your evening class on time due to transport problems or finishing work on time.)

On the next page, I have included a sample layout for you to record your findings.

If you have access to a computer and feel confident enough, you could put this S.W.O.T. analysis into a table with four sections.

For example:

Strengths.	Weaknesses.
How will I make the best of these?	How will I overcome these?
Opportunities.	Threats.
How will I make the best of these?	How will I overcome these?

If you can't do this, do not worry. Just write your findings out as I have shown you on the previous pages.

The main thing is that you have thought about these points and looked at where they fit into your life and how you can plan a way forward in your development.

How I Learn Best.

In this chapter, we will look at learning itself. We will look at what learning is and how this can be achieved. It is important that you understand something of this in order that you do not attend the wrong type of course of learning opportunity. It is important that you enjoy your continuing personal and professional development.

Q. What is learning?

A. Learning is a procedure by which a person gains information from another person.

There are many different ways and reasons for learning.

Do any of those in the examples below ring any bells with you?

> - An ability to absorb information or a skill.
> - Acquisition and absorbing of knowledge or aspect.
> - Gaining knowledge, skills and improving oneself.
> - Receiving new skills – formal or informal.
> - A correct perception of information.
> - An ability to gain more knowledge.
> - To absorb stimuli – store it –process – remember.
> - A form of development.
> - An ability to understand and take in the information given.

Take a moment to think about these.

You may be able to add to the list.

Different Ways of Learning.

We all learn in different ways. However, the basic principles of learning lie in four areas:

- ➢ Motivation.
- ➢ Attention.
- ➢ Retention.
- ➢ Recall.

We will look at each of these in turn.

Motivation.

What is the motivation behind your desire to develop yourself on either a personal or a professional level? In other words, become a learner.

This will depend on your area of work or circumstances.

Ask yourself why **you** have become an adult learner.

Your reason may be **either** a personal need **or** a professional need.

It **may** be both.

Therefore, your MOTIVE can be related to a NEED.

As an adult learner you will most likely be coming back to study voluntarily. We all have something to offer and because of skill and experience in your own area – however limited – *you* have something to offer.

Attention.

Attention is about how people learn and what people learn best. When you attend a training session on a particular subject or topic, you will have a mix of people who will all have different learning styles.

Your training environments may also need to be varied to meet these preferences or at least organised so that it will be acceptable to most people.

You may prefer a more traditional type of learning while others can achieve more in a relaxed group situation.

In all cases, your teacher or trainer should be able to adapt to everyone and be supportive, enthusiastic, and genuinely interested in you all.

Your teacher or trainer should also be aware that you may be returning to learning after a long gap and be sympathetic to this. (This is not easy, as I know from my own experience.)

You should be able to discuss your concerns and find reassurance from your teacher/trainer. If they are aware that some of you have concerns, they should be able to establish a rapport and get you involved from day one.

The important thing is for your teacher/trainer to interact with you and the rest of the group to ensure that they meet **your** needs. This interaction must also be a two-way affair.

Retention and Recall.

RETENTION and RECALL are related to MEMORY.

MEMORY works by using the subconscious or unconscious mind (*for Retention*) as well as the conscious mind (*for Recall*).

It is not easy to remember a random group of numbers – you need some sort of format to link the information to memory.

Learning has not taken place unless there is memory.

In other words, if you can't remember what you have been told then you haven't actually learned anything.

You should find that the teacher/trainer keeps going back over certain points and may feel bored by this. It is important that the main points are reviewed as this is how you will increase your understanding. Otherwise, conscious recall fades. In addition, your teacher/trainer needs to ensure that you understand and that learning has taken place.

Therefore, the key to RECALL is repetition and revision.

If you understand WHY something is done in a certain way, or why something happened, then information will be placed in the memory. Learning will follow.

You may not have just left school or a course of formal learning. You may be a more mature learner who wants or needs to increase skills and knowledge. The effects of ageing must not be underestimated.

However, memory can be improved with use.

You can stimulate memory by using various methods.

Pattern notes such as key words, visual images, connection /linking/network are helpful.

A combination of these, together with frequent reviews will aid **Memory** and so **Retention** and **Recall**.

Feed in the facts and pause to allow your subconscious mind time to absorb the information.

Your teacher/trainer must maintain your attention in order for you the learner, to be able to remember, and subsequently recall, that knowledge.

The key to this is **Motivation.**

Of course one way to keep yourself motivated, and for your teacher/trainer to keep you motivated, is to have regular constructive feedback on how you are doing.

It is important that you know when you have made progress. I know this from my own experience, both as a learner and a teacher/trainer. If, at the start of the learning programme, you are given encouragement in the shape of some small achievement, then you will stay positive.

The goals you are set within the programme must be SMART. We will be looking at this in a later chapter when we come to construct a Personal Action Plan but briefly this means:

Specific.

Measurable.

Achievable.

Realistic.

Time-constrained.

If any of these are not present, the goals or targets are not SMART and you won't achieve your targets and progress.

If the content is hard to understand, make sure that you ask for clarification. Do not be shy.

Either you, your employer or the government through funding has paid good money for this programme of learning.

A variety of activities will address the learning styles of all the learners; will maintain motivation and subsequently, attention, retention of knowledge and recall.

Learning will have taken place. You will have learned something and in the process pushed back, just a little bit, the boundaries of your knowledge. You will have developed.

Learning therefore, is acquiring a knowledge or skill; it involves committing new knowledge to memory.

This would bring about a change in you as a person, which is not simply the result of growth or maturity.

Learning is the development of new knowledge

OR

the ceasing of old knowledge in order to acquire new qualities.

(Riding a bike is learning – growing tall is not learning.)

Task:

Take a moment to think back to one of your learning experiences.

Using the blank sheet overleaf, describe the content (learner activity) and analyse it using the following criteria:

What was the activity?

Why you were undergoing the activity?

What did you learn from the experience?

Why do you think this was?

What aspects did you find pleasant / positive?

What did you not like and why?

How easy did you find it?

How have you changed because of the learning experience?

Was the period of time the right length?

A Learning Activity I Have Experienced.

(Use the space below to jot down some notes or use a notepad.)

Now we will look a little more into the various reasons for learning. As we said earlier, learning is motivated by a need.

Some of these include:

- ➢ To gain qualifications.
- ➢ To gain specific knowledge.
- ➢ To develop yourself (expression).
- ➢ A purposeful use of time.
- ➢ Social & personal safety.
- ➢ Expand job opportunities.
- ➢ Gain independence.
- ➢ A sense of achievement.
- ➢ Income – better pay.
- ➢ Establish confidence.
- ➢ Self-reliance.

These reasons will vary at different times of life and to suit different needs at that time.

You will find that some of the more positive or pleasant aspects of learning can be confidence. In research, which I undertook some years ago, I interviewed a cross section of mature adults who, as mature learners, had different learning experiences.

The main theme, which came out of their learning, was confidence. They all felt more confident as they grew and developed; not only in their job or knowledge base but also in themselves because of acquiring that knowledge and achieving something, which in most cases, they had never thought to be able to do. They felt more in control.

(Lifelong Learning: A View from the Coal Face. Marsh 2011)

Learning Styles.

How do you prefer to learn? Think about it for a moment.

There is a more detailed Learning Styles questionnaire for you to complete later. For now, list what you think is how you prefer to learn.

From your experiences briefly list a couple of your favourite ways of learning. Use your notepad.

Now complete the checklist below. Does it match what you thought was how YOU liked to learn?

Type of learning.	Enjoy.	Do not enjoy.	Give an example of learning situation.
Reading -making notes- (often called self-supported learning).			
Finding out for yourself. Discovering things.			
Learning by 'doing'. Taking part in an activity.			
Instruction or watching a demonstration of how something should be done.			
Taking part in a discussion or completing a question paper.			

D.A Kolb (1971) and Mummford & Honey (1982) – have all developed Learning Style Inventories in order to identify strengths and weaknesses in the process of development of self.

Kolb's Learning Cycle centres on learning by experience, followed by a reflective phase to think about incidents, which have taken place and why they happened. Following this would be the opportunity to apply new ideas and to compare the outcome with the previous experience.

Kolb's Learning Cycle therefore consists of four key areas:

Reflective observation. (Where you reflect on what skills you need in order to develop and achieve your goals.)

Abstract concepts. (Where the ideas are formed. How you are going to meet those needs.)

Application of ideas. (Putting ideas into practice.)

Concrete experience. (Learning by experience.)

After this, you will go back to reflective observation where you review what you have learned, what you have achieved, and what you still need to do.

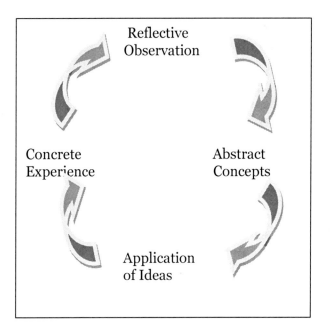

Reflective
Observation

Concrete
Experience

Abstract
Concepts

Application
of Ideas

The cycle can be started at any point. The important thing is to reflect on the experience and learn from it.

At this reflection and evaluation stage, you will review your aims and objectives and identify if they have been met. If not, the cycle starts over again.

If you are to absorb:

KNOWLEDGE. Then there must be

UNDERSTANDING. You will then gain

SKILLS. This in turn will change

ATTITUDES.

Your learning needs will then have been met.

Mumford and Honey then developed what they saw as the main four learning styles:

- ➢ Activists.
- ➢ Reflectors.
- ➢ Theorists.
- ➢ Pragmatists.

The implications of these styles means that we need to choose a learning style, which will allow us to learn from the experience.

After all, if we like being active and doing things we are going to get bored if all of our learning involves being stuck behind a desk and someone talking to us, or being expected to read a book and take notes when we hate that kind of learning.

Activists are practical.

They like to learn with activity and discussion. Activists enjoy presentations, role-play, and games. They enjoy taking part in things and doing practical things in which they interact with others.

Reflectors, as the term implies, prefer quieter ways of learning.

They enjoy research and set reading. Although they lean towards group discussion (this involves reflecting what other people have said), they also enjoy self-study, set reading and doing assignments. They respond to a programme of learning with a structured format. They also lean towards site visits.

Theorists have some of the same leanings as Reflectors.

They like group discussion and enjoy the didactic or instructional type of learning.

Self-study, experiments, lectures and research also fit into the Theorist style.

Pragmatists, as the name suggests, are of a more practical nature.

They enjoy projects and practical demonstration. A Pragmatist will respond to the chalk and talk style of teaching/learning. They lean towards case studies but enjoy the more didactic type of learning as well.

It is quite usual to have more than one style.

The checklist below will make you think about how you like to learn best. This is not hard and fast as over time we all change as we develop and what suits you now may not be the same in a few years time.

It is interesting though, to see what suits you now.

Complete the check-list, giving a score of 1 -4 with 1 being your most liked and 4 being your least liked.

Learning Preferences.	1.	2.	3.	4.
Completing an assignment.				
Listening to tapes/CD.				
Bouncing ideas off people. (Brainstorming)				
Looking at a case study/example.				
Formal discussions.				
Counselling as either a counsellor or patient.				
Instruction/Demonstration.				
Informal discussion.				

See how your learning preferences fall.

Learning Methods	1.	2.	3.	4.
Expert panel of specialists.				
Drama groups.				
Taking part in an experiment.				
Watching films.				
Informal group discussion.				
Fishbowl learning (where one group observes another).				
Group tutorials /feedback.				
Team tasks.				
Games.				
1:1 Tutorial/feedback.				
Individual tasks.				
Lecture.				
Lesson.				
Problem solving.				
Programmed learning.				
Projects.				
Practice.				
Practical.				
Reading.				
Role play.				
Research.				
Step by step discussion.				
T.V.				
Trial and error.				
Video recording.				
Work cards.				
Work sheets/exercises.				

You will be able to see from your results which learning styles you *don't* like even though you prefer a variety of others to varying degrees.

This is quite usual. However, it is likely that you will have a stronger preference for way of learning than another, and will need to work at the others.

If you are not learning and developing in a classroom or company training situation you may be doing your learning through on-line courses, with or without an on-line tutor, or simply by following subjects of interest via the Internet or books. If so, you will be able to choose exactly your own preferred way of learning.

However, this method of what we call Open and Distance Learning (O.D.L.) can be lonely, as you do not interact with other people. On the other hand, if you are combining this way of learning with a more formal approach, then you have the best of both worlds to keep you motivated.

If you have access to the Internet – World Wide Web – you may like to look up the following link on Learning Styles:

http://www.brainboxx.co.uk/a3_aspects/pages/vak_quest
.htm

Remember:

Knowledge must be – absorbed; stored; processed; - and most importantly – remembered.

In this chapter, you have looked at:

> ➢ How to complete a S.W.O.T. Analysis.
> ➢ What I know now.
> ➢ What I need to know in the future.
> ➢ How will I learn what I need to know?
> ➢ What will stop me doing this?

You have travelled a long way on your own personal journey as you work towards achieving your goals in life.

Time Management.

You may have read in various articles and publications about time management. But what do we mean by time management skills? How do we develop these?

In this chapter, we will look at:

> ➢ A definition of 'time'.
> ➢ Good practice.
> ➢ A case study of past practice, using schedules for three working days, and one weekend day.

We will also look at how you can manage your own time in terms of:

> ➢ Task jumping.
> ➢ Indecision.
> ➢ Poor delegation.
> ➢ Interruptions.
> ➢ Distractions.
> ➢ Reluctance to say no.
> ➢ Taking excessive work home.

(Does any of the above ring a bell?)

As part of Continuing Personal and Professional Development you not only need to know how to manage your time; you need to have the tools to develop good practice in order that you keep to your goals and targets.

Development activities don't just happen. They cannot be slotted in when you have a spare minute. They must be planned and programmed into your week.

'I don't have time,' I can hear your say, 'I am very busy.'

If you find yourself thinking this, look back to the chapter on Winners and Losers and see what it says about people who always say they don't have time.

Yes, we are all busy and have responsibilities and things we have to do. The world seems to be moving and spinning around much faster than it used to not so long ago.

I personally believe that this is a prime cause of stress.

But I am also aware that good time management not only relieves stress, allowing pockets of relaxation throughout the day, but that it also enables the task to be completed without adverse effects on others.

When I examined and analysed my own time management practice some years ago, the analysis of my own practice covered a variety of days, which in turn provided a different mix of the types of time on these days. Including an extra weekday into the analysis gave a balanced picture, as the scope of my work at that time varied according to the needs of the business.

My analysis of my personal time management explored how I executed my plan and the effects of changes to the planned day. I will share some of my findings as I feel that providing a real life example will help to put things into perspective.

It can be done. It is the key to releasing your potential.

What is Time?

Time is a gift or a present.

Professor John Adair (1993) who has written much on time management says:

> 'Time is a precious resource.'

He advocates the ten principles of time management, the first of which is to 'develop a personal sense of time'. This may not sound an obvious thing to do but in fact, it makes sense.

He gives '30 ways to make more time'.

John Adair also explores the **concept** of time, concluding that it is many things, but that it is actually something, which is free.

The **next** second is in the future – the **last** second is in the past – **this** second is the 'present', not to be wasted.

Good planning is the key to effective time management and keeping hold of the 'present', which you have been given.

An Examination of Good Practice.

I had followed the Keytime Framework system for some years before embarking on this analysis of my own time. This [Keytime Framework] system consisted of a comprehensive personal management file with numerous sections. Although it seemed cumbersome at first, once I was into the swing of things I found it useful to have everything under one roof so to speak. With a yearly planner; monthly planner; weekly planner; contacts section; a section for project management; a section for keeping track of expenses etc. not much was left to chance.

My personal experience in using this system fine-tuned my previous system, which relied heavily on memory and numerous lists. Does this sound familiar?

Subsequently, logging my time manually became second nature; thus improving and making my time management more efficient.

On the downside, I eventually concluded that you could spend so much time filling in all these different sections that the practice itself became, to a certain extent, non-productive. The key really is moderation in all things and using a system which fits your current lifestyle or job situation.

Organisation, method and the recording of tasks keeps control of time. It is necessary to be aware that recording tasks is, in itself, time consuming (see above); it must be built into the day in such a way that it is an ongoing process and second nature. This is good management and reduces the task.

It is essential to prioritise tasks, but non-urgent tasks can be moved around as required throughout the day. Although prioritising sounds easy, if there are many demands on 'time', more time can be spent in debating how to cope with all the tasks. By working through systematically, delegating where possible and only taking on a realistic number of tasks (with a realistic time scale), you can make valuable time available.

Prior to carrying out this analysis, I had used time management techniques for a few years. My life gradually streamlined into various compartments. With family responsibilities not being as onerous as they had previously been, there was more opportunity for discretionary time.

Setting up a framework facilitated this. From a professional viewpoint, I find that colleagues recognise organisation.

However, being organised and thorough has its drawbacks and can be a two-edge sword; quickly leading to requests for help from others as a matter of course. These requests for help and appropriation of extra tasks should not detract from those very tasks being allocated to the correct recipient, if necessary. However, all too often, they do.

In other words, by being time efficient and appearing to have more time, more tasks can be loaded onto you instead of going to another who really should be given the work to do. This applies to a family situation as much as a professional one.

Gentle assertiveness at various times *did* direct some tasks to their correct destination, thus preserving a well-balanced allocation of time.

On a family basis, the word 'study' is discouraging to others; it is best to use it only when needed. In my own practice, following the lifelong learning path has only been possible by quietly fitting study hours into the framework, which I set up. The discretionary time within the weekly framework must be managed well. In pursuit of your own goals, you will make sacrifices in other areas, which is not always acceptable. The effects of these sacrifices are not always apparent until the time is past and it is too late.

As I reflect on what I wrote those many years ago, I am also reflecting on the effects of some sacrifices which I have made.

Take a moment to think about your life.

Think about sacrifices you make on a personal level, which may be preventing you from following development activities in areas, which you would like to follow.

Make a note below.

....

....

....

Do you take on too much? Do people expect too much of you because you are always willing and always do a good job? Are you organised? Do you keep a diary?

Food for thought!

We will now move on to the next topic of analysing time management.

An Analysis of Time Management.

'Time' can be broken down into three categories:

> ➢ Prescribed time.
> ➢ Maintenance time.
> ➢ Discretionary time.

We will look at each of these in turn.

What is Prescribed Time?

Prescribed time means things you have to do such as going to work, looking after family.

My own life was prescribed around the needs of the business and family responsibilities. I was travelling across the UK as part of the working day. Changes in arrangements with clients and learners often meant that maintenance time and discretionary time changed to prescribed time.

What is Maintenance Time?

Maintenance time is time you spend looking after yourself; shopping, making meals, getting your hair done etc.

This varies according to prescribed time. You tend to fit these tasks in depending on what your work constraints are. In my own case, it had precedence over discretionary time due to family responsibilities. Using outside help for household needs (a cleaner) reduced my maintenance time, allowing me to maintain discretionary time at the necessary level.

What is Discretionary Time?

As the name suggests, discretionary time is time which you have available to do as you please. Your spare time.

I attended a fitness centre. This activity, although located within my discretionary time was, largely prescribed as it was very expensive not to attend on a regular basis.

However, the choice is there – to go or not to go. If there was a need for a little more rest combined with an earlier start on studies, then the option was there. I had a choice. My decision to sometimes not study on a Sunday also enhanced my discretionary time. This allowed me a family day.

An analysis of daily schedules in a flexible working pattern.

Wednesday 21st October.

Prescribed Time.	7h 15 mins.
Maintenance Time.	6h 50 mins.
Discretionary Time.	2h 40 mins.

Due to my travel arrangements for the following day – Thursday – on College business, I had to bring forward the shopping day for my elderly parents. This in turn, meant that I had a later start to my evening, which therefore had the effect of reducing my discretionary time.

As I had to leave work early in order to fit in parental tasks, I felt unable to make a slightly later start in college, which was possible as we managed our own caseloads and time.

Therefore, I did not go to the gym at 06:30am, as was my usual practice at that time. This [shopping] arrangement cut into my discretionary time somewhat; it was a fortnightly event (formerly weekly).

My course development work went as planned; an unscripted meeting with my line manager brought previous work back into focus. We discussed a provisional time for a 'New Contract' meeting on Friday.

My management of the demands on my time was:

Task Jumping.	Yes - but very urgent tasks completed on arrival.
Indecision.	No.
Poor delegation.	No.
Interruptions.	Yes, but welcomed.
Distractions.	Yes – I worked in an open-plan office. There was sunlight on PC screen in spite of part blinds.
Taking excessive work home.	No, this rarely occurs. I use my time to study.

Thursday 22nd October.

Prescribed Time.	7h 50mins.
Maintenance Time.	4h 25mins.
Discretionary Time.	4h 20min.

I was scheduled to travel some distance for a late morning appointment. Therefore, I was able to take advantage of this situation and have a little extra sleep in the morning.

However, due to the timing, I was unable to go to the gym/fitness centre. It was unusual to have one appointment only.

Normally I would have had two appointments and arrive home very late in the evening.

The earlier arrival home in the late afternoon, gave me a chance to catch up with my family and have some relaxation.

My management of the demands on my time was:

Task Jumping.	No.
Indecision.	No.
Poor delegation.	No.
Interruptions.	Yes. Due to limited conditions in the retail store, privacy for feedback/tutorial was limited.
Distractions.	Yes. See above.
Taking excessive work home.	No, this rarely occurs. I use my time to study.

Friday 23rd October.

Prescribed Time.	7h 30mins.
Maintenance Time.	6h 25mins.
Discretionary Time.	4h 30mins.

This was a mixed day. I was keeping things on hold ready for the planned meeting the following morning. After an informal discussion with my colleague, the meeting was re-scheduled for the afternoon. In the event, it took place on the following Monday as my line manager became caught up in other matters.

I completed my task schedule and then ignored it and moved onto development work. It became apparent that what I regarded as important to me is *either* not always what I *should* regard as important *or else* those important tasks were not so critical initially. Only tasks that had to be completed.

I was working in a very autonomous way where I could allow my impulses and freedom to choose, motivate my choice. I was then in control.

I was able to visit family (mother) with newspapers. As my father was 'helping' my husband with the central heating problem, I was able to have an undisturbed chat with Mum. I therefore stayed later than planned.

It was very pleasant. I was home in time to keep track of the household accounts and work on my CPD. (My discretionary time ate into my planned maintenance time but not to adverse effect.)

It was still a quiet period in college.

My management of the demands on my time was:

Task Jumping.	Yes - but very urgent tasks completed on arrival.
Indecision.	No.
Poor delegation.	No.
Interruptions.	Yes, but welcomed.
Distractions.	Yes. It was an open plan office. Sunlight streamed onto my PC in spite of part blinds.
Taking excessive work home.	No, this rarely occurs. I use my time to study and ensure that when in College, I keep as far as possible to the standard hours.

Saturday 24th October.

Prescribed Time.	None.
Maintenance Time.	5h 50mins.
Discretionary Time.	11h 45 mins.

At the time, I was in the habit of keeping Saturdays free for CPD/study. This was my discretionary time, where I could pursue my own goals.

However, the very nature of the work entailed target setting and self-discipline. Therefore, this discretionary time changed into self -imposed prescribed time,

This in turn sometimes overruled my attendance at the fitness centre and dealing with those household chores, which could not be delegated to outside help.

Discretionary time changed into prescribed time, which in turn ate into maintenance time. Long term, this is not a good thing, but in order to provide for long-term needs, it was essential in the short term.

My management of the demands on my time was:

Task jumping.	Yes, but it was my discretionary time that was being 'jumped'.
Indecision.	No.
Poor delegation.	No.
Interruptions.	Yes. Having to remember to load the washing machine.
Distractions.	Yes, Husband arrived home early from work. However, I should not be irritated as he took over the Washing Machine/Tumble Dryer chores, which I had forgotten about.
Taking excessive work home.	No. Not applicable.

Conclusions From the Analysis.

Having looked at my own management of time and referring to various books and articles, it became clear to me that time management is a tool, a tool, which must be continually polished.

There are many schools of thought on the subject of how time can be managed. They have a common theme running throughout, as reference to text indicates. By following the practice of keeping detailed records, it is easy to identify areas for improvement. These improvements could be in the more efficient allocation of time or tasks, as the areas where time is simply wasted become apparent.

At the time of this analysis, I had compiled the highlighted schedules on the college-based desktop PC using pre-installed software. It was useful not only for appointments but also for planning various tasks, which had to be completed.

However, while this calendar-scheduling programme was beneficial, it was relegated to a stand by status when I was working out in the field or at home.

As the same programme was not available at all times on various types of hardware, with file transfer unavailable at that time, the upkeep of a paper-based diary was necessary. I had to update the computer in retrospect with the work I had completed while out of the office.

In that situation, the software programme served as a reference record only, with the time for those hours I spent out of the office being managed manually on a paper-based system.

In either case, whatever method is used, actually recording a daily schedule highlights how time is allocated and spent.

In subsequent years, I continued to work in the field of work-based learning for another organisation. Even though technological advances made it possible to keep details of appointments on a mobile phone or other hand-held appliances and mobile computers, colleagues and I certainly found that a good old-fashioned diary was the best way to keep a paper based record of appointments and tasks.

My own experience demonstrated that as the recording of tasks becomes second nature, it is not time consuming and serves to keep a clear mind.

This in turn allowed for greater efficiency, which impacted positively on others who may have been affected by the schedule.

Stressful situations were minimised.

The examination of daily schedules indicated that there was a wide disparity in the types of tasks undertaken with very little precious discretionary time.

It became clear from my research and experience, that some method of scheduling tasks – preferred by the user – is an essential tool in the management of time.

A Time Management Activity.

Do you keep a diary? Perhaps you are not in a job role where you have to make appointments with clients or schedule in meetings. If you work in the craft trades where you have a variety of customers, you will have to complete a work sheet for each job you have worked on.

How do you remember what you have done in a day?

How do you remember how many hours you spent on 'Job A' or 'Job B'? You may have had to leave 'Job A' for a while to let the paint dry or put it down for a more urgent one and move on to another.

Not all organisations have computerised systems. Many mobile traders keep all their records in a big A4 book, which lives in their van. Their van is their office.

If you work in an office, you will have certain duties, some of which have to be carried out by a certain time; otherwise, the workflow of the department could be endangered.

If you don't write down what you have to do and keep records, you will soon come unstuck.

Using whatever planning aid you prefer – a diary, notepad etc. – keep a record for one week. You might find it a bit tedious but it is a good discipline and will make you think.

At the end of the day or week, look at the following:
- ➤ Task jumping.
- ➤ Indecision.
- ➤ Poor delegation.
- ➤ Interruptions.
- ➤ Distractions.
- ➤ Reluctance to say no.
- ➤ Taking excessive work home.

Start by listing tasks you have to do in the day. (This could be making the tea, sweeping up, collecting, and taking the post, cashing up, issuing work to your team etc.)

You may find it useful to draw up your worksheet or diary into columns. Morning, afternoon and evening and rule it off with time slots.

At the end of each day, take a few minutes to analyse how you spent your day.

Which of the tasks you had planned to do, did you complete?

Which tasks did you complete on time?

Did you make any mistakes?

Why was this?

Was it your fault or the fault of the information given to you? Were you being careless?

If you didn't complete on time why was this?

Did someone wasting your time distract you?

Were you sneaking off for a chat under cover of working?

Which tasks had to be added on to the next day's list?

Which tasks were a waste of time and could have been done more efficiently with better planning?

The list goes on but by now, you should be getting the idea.

Using Time Efficiently.

Lists, lists and more lists. Yes, they are important. It is only by organisation & method that you will make best use of time.

Each evening before you go home – or first thing in the morning –; make a list of what you have to do in the day.

Then put them in order of priority.

Anything with a deadline, time-scale, or anything marked 'urgent' should be Number One.

If there are two Number Ones then you have to make a decision which to do first. It may be that you get the least favourite out of the way first.

On the other hand, you may decide to do the one, which will take the shortest time first. If you have to pass the job on to someone else or another department, then you will need to take that into consideration.

After this, you will look at the order of importance. If you are waiting for a part or component to come in before you can finish the task, you may want to get it as far along as possible so that it can be finished quickly when the part comes in. It depends on the circumstances. Sometimes you will need to discuss this with your supervisor or manager.

Every day there are routing tasks to be done. If you are the 'newbie', it might be your job to make the tea.

Do you have enough milk? It could be said that this is not only an important task but also an urgent one! However, if you have to go to the shop to buy milk, do not waste time and take the opportunity to linger. Your work-mates/colleagues will not be pleased.

Depending where you are on the ladder, you may be in a position to share out the jobs. In other words, delegate. It is important though, for efficient workflow, that you delegate responsibly.

It is no use handing a task to someone who is not competent to do it. If they need help, you will need to build this into the equation.

It could be, as you read this book, that you are thinking that you know all of this. If so, good. You have already taken some steps towards your professional development. If not, well, I hope that this chapter has helped.

If you do not go out to the workplace then the topics above will still be helpful. They are just as useful and essential to your personal development if you look after a family all day.

In fact, bringing up small children is time-consuming. From my own experience with three small children, I found that being methodical and having a routine made my day go smoother. I was able to snatch some 'me time' to do some gardening or read a book.

As in the workplace, I made sure that there was a place for everything and everything was in its place. Putting things away as I went along prevented a build-up of things lying around which needed putting away.

The same applies in an office, workshop or wherever your work is. Apart from anything else, there is a health and safety issue here. If a workplace is not tidy, someone can be hurt if they step on a tool or piece of equipment, which should not have been left out.

In addition, a task takes longer if tools or equipment have to be cleaned or re-set before they can be used.

In the workplace, be methodical. Gather all you need for a job in one go as far as possible. Don't waste time by getting one piece of equipment or an item you need and then having to go back for another when you could have done it all in one go.

Some good practice tips and tricks in using time efficiently.

1. Planning.

- Using to-do lists.
- Post-it-notes.
- Using the planner on the wall.
- Using a diary. These are available with a full week across two pages or with a day to a page to name just a few.
- Some planners can be used with a special whiteboard pen, which can be wiped off.
- Personal organiser e.g. Filofax.
- Electronic planners.

2. Communication.

Talk to your team members. This is important as misunderstandings are minimised.

Talk to someone if you have a problem with a task. Much better to ask before you waste too much time and material trying to sort it out yourself if it is beyond you.

Be polite. Be flexible and helpful but don't be afraid to say no if you really can't help. Otherwise, you can easily be 'put upon'. Perhaps you are the one they ask because you are always organised, but as we saw earlier, this can lead to stress.

Moving on.

As you become more organised and effective, this will be noted. You might not think it but as your manager and colleagues work with you and around you, they will be observing how organised and efficient you are. This can only lead you to gradually taking another step up the ladder.

After you have monitored your practice in managing time, think back to where you where in this respect before you started to read this chapter.

Have the topics and suggestions been useful?

Could you do better?

Did any of the points mentioned ring any bells?

Are you going to use your time more efficiently?

Can you use your time more efficiently?

Keep up, keeping your diary. Add in your personal commitments so that you keep a good balance.

Make your diary or planner one of the most important tools you have.

Check if you are completing tasks on time. Ask your boss for feedback. He or she will be pleased that you want to improve.

Say no if you are busy and are asked to help someone; but have a good reason for not helping, or you will be labelled as inflexible.

Do it right first time!

Otherwise, you will be stressed.

We have now completed the chapter on time management where we looked at:

> ➤ A definition of 'time'.
> ➤ Good practice.
> ➤ A case study of past practice, using schedules for three working days and one weekend day.

We examined the different types of 'time'; how various factors impinge on our planned use of time and ways of making better use of time so that we can reach our goals.

Take a break now while you digest all this knowledge.

In the next chapter, we will look at Stress Management.

Stress Management.

What do we mean by stress?

We often hear someone saying:

'I am stressed!' Are they really? On the other hand, are they just under extreme pressure.

If you are to manage your personal and professional development effectively, you need to be able to recognise and manage stress.

In this chapter, we will look at:

> ➢ What stress is.
> ➢ How it occurs.
> ➢ Some sources and causes of stress.
> ➢ A look at your own life.
> ➢ How you can manage stress.

Much of this chapter is based on research I undertook for my degree some years ago. The BA (Hons) Professional Studies in Education degree was a new one. It fell into the Continuing Professional Development (CPD) framework.

The key element of the course was the module on the process of professional development. This indicated its importance. It doesn't just happen.

Much of what I learnt in this course also related to aspects of vocational learning where developing self and performance is an integral part.

If you are undertaking a vocational programme, you will be able to pinpoint these areas.

I was able to bring forward this good practice into my teaching practice and delivery, to enable my learners to gain the knowledge and understanding needed for good practice and competency.

What is Stress?

> 'Stress is a reaction, physical, mental, or emotional, to demands or changes in your life'
> *(Permanente 1996 P1)*

Another explanation could be explained as follows:

> 'Stress occurs when the pressures upon us exceed our resources to cope with these pressures' *(Changing Times 1997 P1)*

There are many articles and books on the subject of stress. The indicators are that what is beneficial for one e.g. working under pressure, can be harmful for another, and be acute distress.

Therefore, in seeking to analyse stress, it becomes apparent that there is no stereotype definition. Acceptable stress levels vary with each individual. Indeed, they are dependent on individuals' needs and preferences, *at any point in time.* This indicates that what may not have been stressful some years ago, could be stressful some years later due to changing conditions and factors in a person's life.

What is clear, is that stress occurs when pressure becomes more than is acceptable.

At this point, it is counterproductive.

There is a difference in stress and pressure.

Pressure is being stretched – but within the capacity of the individual.

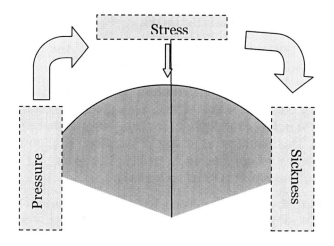

Stress occurs when pressure becomes more than acceptable. It occurs when the optimum level is reached.

Many people work well under pressure and indeed produce their best work under these conditions. However, stress (distress) is counterproductive.

Pressure can turn to stress not only over workload problems; it could be work conditions, which impinge or have an adverse effect on personal life. A build-up of an unresolved problem may result in a seemingly unimportant incident being the trigger for acute distress.

This incident may reflect back to psychological problems or feelings previously buried.

A Critical Examination.

It is important to realise that some of the perceived solutions to stress are in fact reactions.

For example, a common 'solution' is to have a cigarette, a glass of wine, or a stiff drink. This gives us comfort but does not in fact contribute to the long-term management of stress. This *solution* is in fact a *reaction*. It allows us to hide away and not face up to reality. The reality is that the cause of the problem must be identified.

In contrast, regular physical activity contributes to a feeling of well-being and in the long term helps the body to store resources. These resources can be released as required, to cope with the pressures of modern life.

Regular physical activity can include gardening, cleaning brass ornaments, etc., which allow a feel-good factor to emerge and put us back in control. Better by far is a regular attendance at the gymnasium – which is not dependent on the weather – supported by a 'buffer' or mentor. The facility to confide in, or bounce off someone who can take a more pragmatic view, is invaluable.

Good nutrition is important, and to this end, apart from a generally healthy diet, many advocate taking a regular vitamin supplement. This may change with the onset of years, as the body needs a different mix of vitamins and minerals at various times of life.

The opportunity to listen to music in total peace may not often arise in the home. The layout of rooms and family demands has an effect on this. I found that one solution was to compensate by listening to Classic FM in the car whilst travelling. As I travelled a lot at the time of my research, this facilitated a feeling of well being and calm. Many use essential oils in a vaporiser to spread calm and relaxing perfumes into the air.

Over the years, you will find that you change. You may find that you have mellowed somewhat. This could be due to some extent to the actions, which you take to manage stress.

Changes in workplace policies and departmental changes may result in detrimental affects to your personal life. This is quite common. If you have resentments and frustrations at work that is the inevitable result.

You may find yourself feeling that you are being steered down a route, which you don't really want to take. In order to return to the status quo there would be no option but to follow this path. You would be in 'flight' mode.

Eventually, if you cannot accept the changes, things will inevitably come to a head, forcing you to view the whole situation objectively, however painful the process. You may then realise that 'fight' was the answer.

What is more important is that you accept things and take a long-term view while balancing all the issues.

At times like this, a mentor or someone in whom you can trust and confide is invaluable in enabling you to reach a plateau in your feelings. You will notice that I mentioned a long-term view. As you are taking control of your life and learning, it is possible to put these distractions into perspective until things can change.

Sources and Causes of Stress.

In working life, the individual does not always have control over the causes of stress. Some companies take the view that it is not their problem. In contrast, other companies provide state of the art fitness facilities in an effort to redress the adverse effects of the pace of life and environment today. They recognise the part which good health and regular exercise plays in improved performance, for the organisation and the individual. *(Marshall&Cooper 1981)*

Before addressing stress and its effects, it is necessary to acknowledge the cause. i.e. cause and effect.

> Why?
> What?
> When?
> Where?
> How?
> Who?

Once you have identified these, and *only then*, can you examine and apply a solution. In managing stress, it is important to identify between *managing* (coping) and *reacting* to it, i.e. fight, or flight.

In efforts to analyse stress earlier, it became apparent that the cause of stress might be found in the make-up of the individual. The source, therefore, will vary according to each individual(s) trigger(s) and threshold.

One major cause of stress is that it is largely a taboo subject. It is fashionable today to have counselling for all sorts of ills, in preference to using our own personal well of resources. However, for many people there is a fear of being labelled as unstable. Bottling up is, in itself, counter-productive as there is no release of pressure.

Fear of losing a job or promotion is uppermost in the minds of many. The financial worry can lead to a loss of both perspective and effectiveness for the individual concerned.

> 'Failure of the individuals to take responsibility for self-management of their own learning and development and their consequent loss of confidence and ability, results in their anxiety over their employability.' *(IPD October 1998 P.3)*

In

> 'Walker v Northumberland County Council, the judge pronounced that the employers' duty of care also extended to protection against psychiatric harm.' *(IPD October 1998 P. 4)*

Life today is vastly different from 100 years ago. Technological advances, far from making life easier, have in fact placed many more demands on individuals and organisations. Much of the subsequent work can be boring and subject to repetition. This, coupled with the ability to produce more to meet increased production targets, can set up the stress cycle. This stress cycle is often aggravated by noisy surroundings.

Adverse working conditions result.

A more common cause of stress is a personality clash. Many firms use psychometric tests in an attempt to build the 'right' team. Although not infallible, they **do** provide a guide to selection.

However, good management and leadership can do more to address many problems. Lack of support in this area can lead to a build up of resentment over a period.

> 'Stress, if continuous, can affect physical, mental, and emotional wellbeing.' *(Kaiser Permenante 1996)*

For this reason, for their effective management, it is important to recognise the sources and causes of stress.

How Stress Can be Managed.

In identifying the sources and causes of stress, it is important to assess where things can be *changed* and where they must be accepted. You can then enter a state of reconciliation using a personal well of inner and more tangible resources to maintain this state.

Many people keep a daily diary to write down their thoughts. (Not the work diary full of things to do.) This emptying of the mind can be therapeutic. The problems thus become less of a problem as a sense of perspective gradually re-asserts itself.

Writing can be therapeutic. Many people vent their feeling in a letter, which they never actually send. Writing things down allows them to give vent to their feelings but in the cold light of day, after a period of reflection, they may well ask themselves if it is worth it and tuck the letter away to be disposed of later.

(On reflection, as I write, I ponder on the adverse effects of responding too quickly and sometimes in anger, to an e-mail; pressing the 'send' button before considering the effect of hasty words. The old saying of 'sleep on it – it will look better in the morning' has its value.)

However, in managing stress, it is important to approach from a two-pronged point of view.

John D Adams (1985) bases his techniques for stress management on not only individual responsibilities but also on organisational responsibilities; focussing the responses to situations on the immediate and long term.

How can you manage stress in your life?

An honest self-examination of the causes of stress in your life leads on to a structured approach to its prevention and the formulation of some solutions.

For myself, I found that with a very full diary it often took a lot of will power to get up very early in the morning and be at the fitness centre for a workout at 06:30am. From experience, I found that this was the best time for me before I became involved in the day. It was time for *me*.

You will find your own solution. It could be walking the dog. You will need to keep to a healthy diet, possibly including a daily vitamin supplement. That is your preference but in the hurly, burly of modern life it is easy to miss vital nutrients.

You must accept that you cannot be super-woman or super-man. You cannot be all things to all men. If you cannot do as much as you would wish around the home, it is not the end of the world.

You may have had a career change or be planning one. You may need to accept that the career change has altered the scope of personal responsibility.

If you have moved into a supervisory or management role in your workplace, you will in effect have 'jumped the fence'. This means that in work, you have to leave personal friendships aside when making decisions; especially unpopular ones.

This can be a hard discipline to follow; sitting on the fence is not an option if you are to supervise or manage effectively. Your success in this area is largely dependent on others' management of you.

You may have attended various fitness centres or gyms over the years. It is common practice to be re-assessed every 6 months and the programme adjusted to suit. Many fitness centres have a pool area for a good swim or gentle splash. This is a good cooling down strategy. It also gives you time to let your thoughts wander and put problems into perspective as you work them out in your mind and put them into the right compartment.

To finish a session by relaxing in the sauna contributes to a feeling of inner cleanliness and fitness.

Experience may show that infrequent attendance leads to an increase in stress levels and less personal effectiveness. You may have a tendency to dwell on trivial matters as they return.

With life expectancy increasing, people are living much longer than hitherto. In addition, for a variety of reasons, parenting often comes later in life than some years ago. People in their middle age who are at a time of life where their bodies – although not their minds – are slowing down, were once regarded as 'the old folk'. They now find that they are what is known as 'the filling in the sandwich' as they strife to care for elderly parents and help with young grandchildren, in addition to their own home and work responsibilities.

It is not easy.

However, you can only do what you can and there are support systems out there. Good time-management and adaptability to changes, will allow you to keep things in your mental compartments.

If you cannot allocate a time of relaxation on a daily basis, then grab those pockets in the day which pop up as and when, and relax. Catnapping helps to re-charge the batteries. The danger point is in being very tired and losing your sense of perspective leading to self-induced stress.

The self-discipline, which you are practicing in other areas, needs to extend to yourself to enable you to look after your own health. *Me* time is important. You have a life. If you are fortunate enough to have an understanding husband/wife/partner who works with you as a team, providing a shoulder to cry on, you are blessed.

Keeping a positive attitude is essential in the management of stress. Kaiser Permanente (1996) advocated 'positive visualization', creating a picture of the desired outcome.

I found by far that the best solution – thanks to a recent innovation in our lives at that time - was to soar up into the hills, riding pillion on our new touring motorbike. After many years absence in the 'saddle' for my husband, I found it wonderfully relaxing to gaze up through the trees at the clouds and blue sky, feeling the wind rushing through the visor to blow away the cobwebs.

It was a perfect opportunity to 'empty the mind' and get away from it all. You will have your own opportunities. Nevertheless, sometimes you have to make them.

Conclusions and Recommendations.

During the research outlined in this chapter, I looked at stress in my own life. After referring to various books and articles, it became apparent that stress is a deeper subject than can be given full justice within *this* short chapter.

Having examined various sources of information and various schools of thought, what did become apparent, however, is that stress is a modern problem; a problem exacerbated by the increasing pace and pressures of modern life together with increases in technology and knowledge.

In order to turn reaction to stress into the management of stress, it is apparent that there is a need for a return to the healthier lifestyle of yesteryear. While recognizing that everyone has a problem – often rooted in a long-forgotten incident – hard work, exercise and a healthy diet, will provide a natural antidote to the pressures of life.

In becoming aware of the different phases of stress, a better understanding of oneself can be achieved. An acceptance of unchangeable situations, coupled with life adjustments where possible, may take away or reduce the causes and effects of stress.

This will allow a more effective management of it; promoting a more positive outlook and subsequent benefits.

In this chapter, we looked at:

> - What stress is.
> - How it occurs.
> - Some sources and causes of stress.
> - A look at your own life.
> - How you can manage stress.

I hope that you now have more understanding of how you can minimise the pressures and subsequent stress in your life, in order that you can continue to release and realise your potential.

There are many articles and books on the subject if you wish to look into it further. You will find these on the Internet, your local library or bookshop.

Take a moment to reflect on this chapter. . . .

You are now ready to move on to constructing a Continuing Personal Development Portfolio.

Personal Development Recording

A Personal Action Plan.

A Personal Development Record.

Taking Stock.

A Personal Development Portfolio.

A Personal Action Plan.

In an earlier chapter, you were asked to complete a Skill scan. You were also asked to think ahead about what you want to achieve in the next 1/3/5 yrs.

In the S.W.O.T. Analysis, you were asked to think about what you would need to do to achieve these aims.

Now that you have worked through more chapters of this guide, think again realistically taking into account your current responsibilities. Think about your short term development needs, your long term development needs, and write the key areas in which you will need training over the next few months or longer term. You need to consider your present job role, where it might develop, what new tasks you might be required to undertake. In addition, if you are working to a National Vocational Qualification (NVQ) you need to think about the units you hope to complete.

Try to put realistic dates into your plan, and discuss it with your manager or assessor at your first review or a family member or friend if that is more appropriate.

The main areas, which you need to have on this plan, are as follows:

- ➢ Key Development Areas-short term/long term.
- ➢ How you will achieve this.
- ➢ Target Date for Completion.
- ➢ Actual Finish Date.

If you are learning informally, you may want to keep an informal record as follows:

Key Development Area (1)-short term/long term.

....

Target Date for Completion...

How I will achieve this? What course do I need?

....

....

Actual Finish Date...

Key Development Area (2)-short term/long term.

....

Target Date for Completion...

How I will achieve this? What course do I need?

....

....

Actual Finish Date...

And so on.

If however you have access to a computer and can draw a simple table, you will probably find that the following is more useful:

Personal Action Plan.	Date of Plan.	Date for Review.
Key Development Areas. How I will achieve this.	Target Date for Completion.	Actual Finish Date.

You will notice that on the plan I have included a space to write the date of the plan and a date for review.

Remember, this is planned learning. We are leaving nothing to chance. It is only by keeping on top of this plan that you will achieve your goals.

Yes, you may well come up against obstacles. You may have to leave your learning at one side to deal with some urgent family matter. If you are allocated time in work, your learning time should be non-negotiable.

That means that you should not be pulled off your agreed study time to deal with problems.

Sometimes what are termed as emergencies are in reality just an urgent problem.

If you are pulled off your study time, make sure that you get it back so that you can catch up.

The same goes for self-study at home. After all, if you were going to an evening class in college and a problem cropped up, no one would expect you to miss college would they. That would be unthinkable. In any case, if you missed college too often, you would be thrown off the course.

Just as we have looked at time management for *you*, you must expect others to use time management and planning skills in order that you can study. It won't happen if you or they treat it as an ad hoc activity. Your learning needs must be respected.

We are now going to look at a Personal Development Record, as this is a crucial part of your development and quest to release and realise your potential.

You are now probably beginning to see how all the pieces of the jigsaw of learning are falling into place.

Don't forget to make sure your targets are SMART!

A Personal Development Record.

On your Personal Action Plan, there was a date for a review.

This is where you review your action plan and reflect on some aspects of your learning so that you can see how you are getting on. If you are undertaking a long course, it is a good idea to review aspects of the full course on a unit/module basis. Otherwise, it is too much to think about and review in one go. This reflective review is part of the Personal Development Record and an important aspect of learning and development. Please give it some time.

What was the task/learning activity?

....

....

Did you meet your target? Y/N

If not, why not? (Write some reasons below.)

....

....

....

....

How did you feel about the learning activity? Did the way of learning suit you?

....

....

....

What did you learn? What were the topics?

....

....

....

What do you feel that you personally have learned from this activity?

....

....

....

How did you feel about what you have learned? Include both the practical and theory parts of the activities.

....

....

....

Where there any problems? Y/N

If so, what did you do about it?

....

....

....

How could you improve?

....

....

....

This is where you re-visit your action plan and revise your target date for an activity if needed.

Remember - Make sure it is:

Specific

Measurable

Achievable

Realistic

Time-constrained

Taking Stock. A Periodic Review of Learning.

Taking stock simply means sitting down and looking back on your Personal Action Plan as a whole. So the target date for review on your Personal Action Plan should be a period of a few months hence. When I was undertaking management studies in a formal learning situation, my tutor carried out this taking stock review.

When undertaking a *variety* of learning activities, this review process wasn't an automatic part of self-study activities; reviews for formal courses however, were carried out by a variety of reviewers depending on the study activity.

Therefore, I continued on my own with this taking stock activity as I found it so valuable. It just brought everything together and was independent of the various courses I was undertaking, which had their own reviews. This was part of my *own* continuing personal development.

I had taken ownership of my own learning and development. This record would go with me wherever I was to work and be a testimony to my commitment to realising my potential on my lifelong learning journey.

Overcoming Problems.

No one says that learning is easy. It isn't. At least not in respect of building it into your very busy life.

Learning should be fun, however. If you are enjoying the way in which you are learning, then you are more likely to stick at it in spite of problems, which will inevitably crop up.

If you are just starting out as a soon-to-be school leaver or a university graduate, you will be well into the swing of timetabling study into your social life. Keep this up. CPD is much easier if you keep records from the start and build on the Record of Achievement with which you left school.

If you are a returner to learning, either from years of not studying while you progressed in your job, or from years spent at home with family care responsibilities, you may well find it daunting to keep up with a course. How can you overcome problems, which will arise from a quite drastic lifestyle change?

➤ Use time management skills. Do not forget your diary or planner.

➤ Priority - No 1 task. Make your learning one of the most important things in your life.

➤ Be focused - keep your eye on the ball. Do not be distracted from your goals.

➤ Keep assessment appointments. Make these a firm appointment, which has priority even if you are not attending a formal college course. Make them non-negotiable with others who want you to change your plans. Learning is fun but it doesn't just happen. You have to make it happen.

➤ Keep to your target dates Make sure that your targets are SMART.

➤ If you miss a target then don't just abandon things. Make a fresh date for completion of that particular chunk of learning.

A Personal Development Portfolio.

What is a 'Portfolio'?

A portfolio is simply a collection of relevant information, which is stored securely.

It can be a ring binder; a box file; stored on a disc; paperless. It is your choice but above all, it must be clearly structured, clearly presented, and easy to follow.

Many organisations have moved over to asking – mainly from higher level employees – that these are kept up but it is never too late to start and if you take one along to a job interview, well, you will impress the interview panel as they will see that you are serious about achieving high standards and want to learn and progress.

I have always found that a ring binder with a clear plastic front pocket is a good choice, both in my work in the vocational area and in my own development activities.

Having a clear front pocket on the ring binder, means that you can slip in a nice cover with your name etc. on it. Don't forget, that at this point, you won't want your organisational details or logo as this is a personal portfolio. (Unless of course your organisation is providing it.) This portfolio will form the record of your learning throughout your working life.

Don't buy the biggest, fattest one on the shelves. They are really hard to open! One about 4cm is sufficient.

You will need a set of file dividers. A set of five should be enough. If you are going to use plastic pockets then you will need to buy an extra wide ring binder and file dividers. Otherwise, the labels will be hidden.

Below is a suggested structure for your Personal Development Portfolio.

Inside front cover put the following details:

Name:

Employer:

Job Title:

Department:

Date of Appointment:

Line Manager:

Member of...

If you are a member of a professional organisation put the details here. I would not advocate putting membership numbers, as these are confidential.

Next, you will need a Contents Sheet. Some packs of file dividers provide one of these. Otherwise, you can hand write or type one up.

It is nice to have everything done on the computer and we all like to show off our IT skills. Most libraries nowadays have computer access quite freely. However, if you don't have access to a computer at home or work and your local library or Learning Centre is not accessible to you, then handwritten documents are fine. Just make sure that they are clean, clear, and easy to read with no spelling mistakes.

That of course goes for paperwork produced on the computer as well. Also, don't rely on the computer spell-checker. Print off and check that the words are the right words!

> *e.g., I **passed** my Level Two Certificate Exam (correct).*
>
> *I **past** my Level Two Certificate Exam (incorrect).*

Contents

1. Personal Details.
Curriculum Vitae. (C.V.)
Job Description.
Employer Information.

2. Occupational/Work Competencies.
Training Record.
S.W.O.T. Analysis.
1/5/10 yr. Objectives.

3. Personal and Professional Development.
Personal Action Plans /Taking Stock.
Personal Development Record.
Employer/Employee Appraisals.

4. Evidence of Achievement.
Certificates.
Course/Workshop Feedback.

5. Evidence of Good Practice.
Professional Updating Activities.

(Here you can insert anything you think is relevant and useful that doesn't fit into the other sections. This will depend on your job role or outside activities.)

Section One - Personal Details.

Section One – Curriculum Vitae.
Using the sample below, write a C.V. Refer back to the previous chapter on compiling a Curriculum Vitae.

Curriculum Vitae of < Name >.

(Also, add any professional designatory letters after your name or a degree.)

Personal Profile. *(Example.)*

I am an organised, enthusiastic, and committed individual who has demonstrated accomplishments in the areas of *<here put whatever relates to you>*.
I am a motivated individual with good communication skills and a flexible attitude who works well in a team. I have contributed in a positive way to the work of my department *< give an example if possible>*. Recently I have *< here insert something positive you have done>*.
My current position as a *< . . . >*, requires me to apply method, attention to detail and interpersonal skills.
In my spare time, I am a member of my local amateur dramatic society, which relies on teamwork.

Include the Personal Profile, which you drafted earlier.

Personal Information.

Address: e-mail:

Tel: Mobile:

Professional Memberships. *(If none, leave out.)*

Include details of any organisations you belong to or professional memberships you have. Remember, your life outside work gives an indication of what you are like as a person. e.g.

June 2008 – to date   Institute of Leadership

and Management. Member.

Education. Training. Professional Qualifications.

Date: (most recent first.) Awarding Body and subject.

> Include details of your Education and Training starting with the most recent first. This is important. If there are hundreds of applicants for a job you want to make sure that your prospective employer can see what you can do *now*; not what you were doing when you left school or before your current job.

> You need to make an impact.

> If you are working towards a qualification, include this before anything you have already achieved. If you are undertaking an apprenticeship which has lots of different parts (e.g. the Technical Certificate or taught part of the course which provides the knowledge and understanding /NVQ/Key Skills etc.) then list the name of the Apprenticeship and then all the components.

> Don't forget to list your GCSE and GCE A-level results – highest grade first.

> Include any achievements from school e.g. Princes Trust Award/ Duke of Edinburgh Award Scheme/Health and Safety or First Aid Certificates.

<u>Employment Experience.</u> *(Most recent first.)*

Include your employment history. Again, start with the last one first for greater impact. (Any part time jobs you had while at school, or before this employment, are very relevant as they show application and flexibility.

Date   **Organisation. Address.**
                            Position.

This involved − *(Here give a general overview of your duties.)*

Achievements. *(Here give any successes your department achieved or targets you reached. Include your personal contribution.)*

Date   **Organisation. Address.**
                            Position.

This involved − *(Here give a general overview of your duties.)*

Achievements. *(Here give any successes your department achieved or targets you reached. Your personal contribution.)*

If it is not long since you left school or worked, don't forget to include any part-time or casual work. What you include in this section depends on your circumstances.

If you are further on in your working life you may want to make the earlier positions briefer.

If you have had a number of part-time or short-term jobs, you could combine them all together by saying for instance:

1998-2003   I worked in a variety of jobs in . . .
This would show that you are flexible and willing to work.

Personal Interests and Activities.

Include any other relevant information about yourself or your achievements, which may not have shown up earlier.

Include brief details of any hobbies or interests.

Here you could include any clubs or organisations of which you are a member. This helps to give your prospective employer a brief insight into you as a person and what other qualities you demonstrate that you could bring to the job role.

References are available on request.

Do not include actual references with a job application unless the job description asks for them. These will be asked for if the employer wants them.

You may be asked to give the names of two referees, who can be contacted if needed. Be sure to obtain their permission first.

Some suitable sources for a character reference would be former teacher, Minister of Religion, a professional person, someone with a good standing in the community.

Signature: Date:

**Don't forget to use a footer with the date inserted so that you know which the latest is when you come to update it. When you do update save it as a new file.

On the following page is a basic outline of what your C.V. could look like.

Curriculum Vitae of A.N.Other

Personal Profile.

> [   ]

Personal Information.
Address.   e-mail.
Tel: Mobile.

Professional Memberships.

Education. Training. Professional Qualifications.
Date.   Awarding Body and Subject
                                  and Grade.

Employment Experience.
Date From – To   **Organisation. Address**
                                  Position.

This involved –

Achievements.

Date From – To   **Organisation. Address**
                                  Position.

This involved –

Achievements.

Personal Interests and Activities.

References are available on request.
Possibly give the name of two referees.

Signature: Date:

Section One cont. Job Description.
Insert a brief overview of your current job. Your employer should have one or there may be something in the staff handbook. It could also be with your current Contract of Employment.

Section One cont. Employer Information.
Include some information about your current employer. You may be able to find this on the Internet if none other is available. It will provide a prospective employer an insight into the organisation for which you work now.

Section Two. Occupational/Work Competencies.
Training Record.
SWOT Analysis.
1/5/10 yr. Objectives.

Section Three. Personal and Professional Development.
Personal Development/Action Plans/Taking Stock.
Personal Development Record.
Employer/Employee Appraisals.

Section Four. Evidence of Achievement.
Certificates. *Include most important and most recent first.*
Include your GCSE/GCE A-level certificates.
Course/Workshop Feedback.

Section Five. Evidence of Good Practice.
Any Professional Updating Activities.

Here you can insert anything you think is relevant and useful that does not fit into the other sections. This will depend on your job role or outside activities.

In this chapter, you have pulled together all the learning in this guide.

From the knowledge and understanding you have gained from the first chapters where you looked at how you learn best; learning styles; the importance of time management; how stress can affect your performance and ways of managing these; you have been able to move on to constructing your own personal action plan and development records.

Not only will these be invaluable in helping you to achieve your goals in life as you release and realise your potential; your portfolio will be a lasting record of the efforts and focus you have put on your own learning and development. It should impress any prospective employer and may give you the edge when it comes to job applications and interview.

In the next and final chapter, we will look briefly, at what an effective learning and development strategy consists of.

This can be adopted by any organisation or individual who seek to improve and upskill in the drive for increasing personal and economic prosperity.

An Effective Learning and
Development Strategy

**Learners to take ownership of
own learning and development**

- Staff Development   Process of Professional
  Session - all staff ⟶ Development

- Personal Audit   Personal Development
                  Plan !

- Personal   Personal Development
  Development   Record-
  Portfolio- ongoing   *with critical reflection of own practice.*

➤ All learners to take responsibility for their own
   learning & development.
➤ Personal Audit.
➤ Where am I now?
➤ Where do I want to be-1 /5/10 years time?
➤ What do I need to do to achieve this?

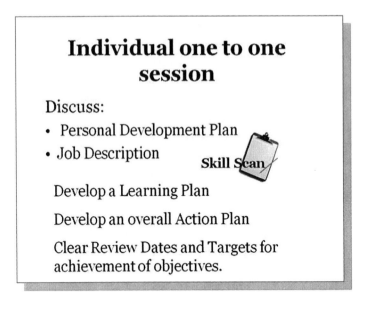

Individual one to one session

Discuss:

- Personal Development Plan
- Job Description

Skill Scan

Develop a Learning Plan

Develop an overall Action Plan

Clear Review Dates and Targets for achievement of objectives.

> ➤ SWOT Analysis.
> ➤ Personal Development Plan.
> ➤ Personal Development Record.

Keep all these in your Personal Development Portfolio (however simple).

Now that you have identified what you need to do, you now need to think about how you are going to achieve your goals – however long-term.

Think about what kind of learning experience you would be happy. Refer back to the chapters about *learning styles* and *how you learn best*. These are important.

Just as important are the different types of resources you need and which will be available to you.

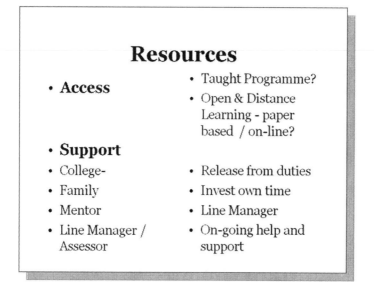

Resources

- **Access**
  - Taught Programme?
  - Open & Distance Learning - paper based / on-line?

- **Support**
  - College-
  - Family
  - Mentor
  - Line Manager / Assessor
  - Release from duties
  - Invest own time
  - Line Manager
  - On-going help and support

Think about what kind of support you will have.

Will your family take over some of your household chores while you study?

Can you free up some study space? It is important that you have somewhere, even if just a corner in the kitchen, where you can study undisturbed and keep your work clean and presentable.

Will your employer/supervisor give you time out in work? If they promise this, will they actually make sure that you get it? If not, your targets are not going to be SMART.

Are you prepared to give up football or your Salsa classes etc? Think about this. If you can still fit these in, then great! You need the activity but if you go to sports five nights a week, you might have to sacrifice just one.

If you do not have formal staff development sessions or you are in the unfortunate position of not being employed, there is nothing to stop you following these basic steps on your own, with a friend or member of your family.

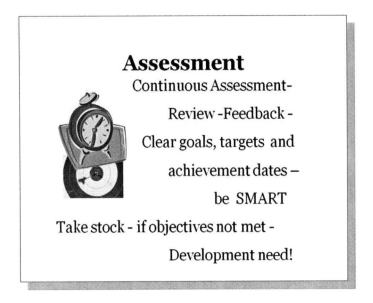

Assessment

Continuous Assessment-

Review -Feedback -

Clear goals, targets and

achievement dates –

be SMART

Take stock - if objectives not met -

Development need!

The important thing is that you continually push back the boundaries – taking one step at a time – to allow you to grow, to release those gifts and skills within yourself, which have not yet flowered fully.

We are nearly at the end of this short guide, which aims to help you to release your potential. This series of guides is based around lifelong learning and personal effectiveness.

To go back to the beginning, we are not only asking:

'What is lifelong learning?' but:

'Why lifelong learning?'

The lifelong learning culture contributes to the releasing and realising of human potential. It is essential for personal fulfilment.

The lifelong learning culture also increases skills. It contributes to the success and quality of organisations and the employability of you, the learner – the stakeholder.

The lifelong learning culture contributes therefore to the economic success and prosperity of the nation as a whole as it becomes more competitive.

Finally:

Lifelong Learning Culture

" education and training regimes which
do not contribute to ....constant
effort of 'personal construction' will
not do very well"

(Arthur Stock in The Learning Society-
Challenges and Trends. Raggat et al 1996.p.21)

References

Adair, J. (1993)	A Guide to Keytime Management System. Topps of England Ltd.
Adams, J.D. 1981	Planning for Comprehensive Stress Management in Cooper & Marshall. Gower.
Allcorn, S. Diamond, M.A. 1997	Managing People during Stressful Times: the psychologically defensive workplace. Quorn Books.
Ask Jeeves (1998)	"what is stress?" www.ask jeeves.com sourced 10 - 19/10/98
Blanchard, L.	The One Minute Manager ©Blanchard Family partnership & Candle Communications Corp.1982/3
Bush & Middlewood (Eds).	Managing People in Education. Paul Chapman.
Changing Times. (1997)	Stress. The Changing Times way to Stress Relief www.stress.com in www.askjeeves.com what is stress? Sourced 14/10/98
Cooper, C.L. & Marshall, J. (1981)	Coping with Stress at Work. Gower.
Cooper, C.L. & Marshall, J. (1985)	Planning for Comprehensive Stress Management. Gower.
Cooper,C.L. & Payne, R.(1998)	Causes, Coping and Consequences of Stress at Work. John Wiley & Sons.
Crawford, M.(1997)	Managing Stress in Education in Bush & Middlewood (Eds): Managing People in Education. Paul Chapman.
Davies, Ellison et al (1990)	Education Management for the 1990's. Longman.

Ellison, L.(1990)	Effective Time Management and Managing Stress in Schools from: Davies B, Ellison et al Education Management for the 1990's Longman.
Honey, P. & Mumford A.(1982)	Learning Styles Questionnaire in Manual of Learning Styles.
HSE (1998)	Stress, the psychological contract and business performance in: Key Facts-Stress at Work Institute of Personnel & Development. October 1998 P1-6
IPD (1998)	Key Facts-Stress at Work Institute of Personnel & Development October 1998 P1-6
Kaiser Permanente.(1996)	Stress www.kpne.com in www.askjeeves.com - what is stress? sourced 10/10/98
Leask, M.	Developing, Planning & School improvement
Terril, I.(1997)	for Middle Management. Kogan Page
Newton, T.(1995)	Managing Stress: Emotion and Power at Work. Sage Publications.
Onken Jnr, W Wass, D.L.(1974)	Management Time: Who has got the Monkey in: Harvard Business review Vol52 No6 Nov/Dec 1974 P5 reprint No 74607
Pinnacle Management Consultants 1993	In Team Building. Kolb Learning Cycle, D A Kolb.
Sime W. E.(1997)	Stress Management, Bio Feedback, and Peak Performance www.unl.edu / in www.askjeeves.com what is stress? sourced 14/10/98
Skills Audit and Feedback.	http://www.surrey.ac.uk/Skills/Pack/iolp.html
Stock A.	The Learning Society. Challenges and Trends. Raggat et al 1996 p21.